Dedications & Other Darkhorses

Lost in the Bonewheel Factory

Copacetic

I Apologize for the Eyes in My Head

Toys in a Field

Dien Cai Dau

February in Sydney

Magic City

Neon Vernacular: New and Selected Poems, 1977–1989

Thieves of Paradise

Blue Notes: Essays, Interviews, & Commentaries

Talking Dirty to the Gods

Pleasure Dome: New and Collected Poems, 1975–1999

Taboo: The Wishbone Trilogy, Part I

Gilgamesh: A Verse Play

Warhorses

The Chameleon Couch

THE EMPEROR OF

WATER CLOCKS

AKAA

THE

EMPEROR

OF

WATER

CLOCKS

FARRAR STRAUS GIROUX / NEW YORK

FARRAR, STRAUS AND GIROUX

18 West 18th Street, New York 10011

Copyright © 2015 by Yusef Komunyakaa

All rights reserved

Printed in the United States of America

First edition, 2015

Library of Congress Cataloging-in-Publication Data

Komunyakaa, Yusef.

[Poems. Selections]

The emperor of water clocks : poems /

Yusef Komunyakaa. — First edition.

pages ; cm

ISBN 978-0-374-14783-9 (hardcover)

I. Title.

PS3561.O455 A6 2015

811'.54—dc23

2015011215

Designed by Quemadura

Our books may be purchased in bulk for promotional,
educational, or business use. Please contact your local
bookseller or the Macmillan Corporate and Premium Sales
Department at 1-800-221-7945, extension 5442, or by
e-mail at MacmillanSpecialMarkets@macmillan.com.

www.fsgbooks.com

www.twitter.com/fsgbooks

www.facebook.com/fsgbooks

1 3 5 7 9 10 8 6 4 2

FOR LAREN

CONTENTS

*

THE EMPEROR OF

WATER CLOCKS

THE LAND OF COCKAIGNE

A drowned kingdom rises at daybreak
& we keep trudging on. A silhouette rides
the rope swing tied to a spruce limb,
the loudest calm in the marsh. Look
at the sinkholes, the sloped brokenness,
a twinned rainbow straddling the rocks.
See how forgiving—how brave nature is.
She drags us through teeming reeds
& turns day inside out, getting up
under blame, gazing at the horizon
as a throaty sparrow calls the raft home.
A wavering landscape is our one foothold.
Are we still moving? This old story
behind stories turns an epic season
a tangle of roses moved by night soil.
The boar, Congo snake, & earthworm
eat into pigweed. The middle ground
is a flotilla of stars, a peacock carousel
& Ferris wheel spinning in the water
as vines unstitch the leach-work of salt,
thick mud sewn up like bodies fallen

into a ditch, blooming, about to erupt.
Water lily & spider fern. I see the tip
of a purple mountain, but sweetheart,
if it weren't for your late April kisses
I would have turned around days ago.

OMENS

Her eyelids were painted blue.
When she closed her eyes the sea
rolled in like a hundred fiery chariots,

leaving behind silence above & below
a thousand years old. He stood beneath
a high arched window, gazing out

at fishing boats beyond the dikes, their nets
unfurled, their offshore gestures
a dance of living in bluish entourage.

He was only the court's chief jester.
What he said & did made them laugh,
but lately what he thought he knew

could cost his polished tongue & royal wig.
He was the masked fool unmasking the emperor.
Forget the revelation. Forget the briny sea.

He had seen the ravishing empress naked
in a forbidden pose. Her blue eye shadow.
Aquamarine shells crusted with wormy mud.

Anyway, if he said half of what was foretold,
the great one would become a weeping boy
slumped beneath the Pillars of Hercules.

THE WATER CLOCK

A box of tooth wheels sits on an ebony hippopotamus
made to count seasons. I show you a sketch of the float,
how it steals wet kisses out of a mouth, the bulbous belly
swollen with hours, my left hand at the hem of your skirt.
How many fallen empires dwell here triggered by a sundial,
revolutions & rebirths? I'm in a reverie again, my face
pressed against the rounded glass wall of the city aquarium
as hippopotami glide slowly through water, in sync to a tune
on my headphones. Why can't I stop intoning the alchemist
who used the clock to go between worlds & turn lead to gold?
A replica of this in a brothel in Athens once counted off
minutes each client spent in a room. If this is a footnote
to how one defines a day, no one knows this timepiece
as well as the superintendent of water debiting farmers.
The dark-green figs ripen under moonlight. Migratory
birds lift from shoulders of scarecrows at sunrise & arrive
in a new kingdom at sunset, true as the clock's escapement
mechanism. The bridge of zodiac signs moves across the top.
A lifetime poises in my fingers on the silver clasp of your bra
as spring's rapaciousness nears. Your slip drops to the floor
& ripples at our feet as a blooming cereus opens.
All the sweet mechanics cleave heaven & earth,
& a pinhole drips seconds through bronze.

THE EMPEROR

The tablet he inherited was encased
in leather, & in sleep he whispered
a decree to conquer the hermaphrodite
on the throne. Acacias touched yellow
to the night & peace reigned a decade.
When he ordered his brother to serve
as his double, his mother said, Son,
your father would have banished you
to the salt mines. The look in his eyes
was what Grotowski tried to capture
at La MaMa, a looped robe at his feet
& baroque notes echoing in his head.
The three double-jointed stuntmen
& master of props were his friends,
& he learned all the pressure points
from the third guard. He was emperor
before a script, a taste for honeycomb
at birth, long before the abominable
oath was tattooed on his forehead.
His brother would face the throng
mornings outside the marketplace
across from the old sacred abattoir

to sing bygones & lines of succession.
This was a place of drawn daggers
& acts of sedition, renown for blood
on stones & laments scribed on air,
& also for wheels drawing water
up rocky inclines to his garden.
He was born to claim his father's
flame trees & the white rhinoceros.
In another life, he could have been
an illustrious actor, a kind word
even for dumb brutes of the forest.
He mastered sublimity & decorum
bathed in the glow of a leading lady,
& the peach brandy & plum bread
he loved was always first tasted
by his double. Questions of fidelity
& bloodline, honor & dishonor, all
went back to Hagar & a gold scepter.
His brother was forbidden a name.
From his court he could see faces
lined up to praise his terraced garden
of shrubs, herbs, ornamental grasses,
& hues to bribe the raven to his door.
He said, Mother, time will forgive me
because I have always loved beauty.

THE FOOL

C'mon, Your Majesty, her brother?
I know the scent of belladonna
can poison a mind, even a king's,
but would you dare to behead
your own nightmares? Now,
I hope you are more than pewter
& pallor. Where is the early heart
I gladly remember from the days
I hailed as your father's cutthroat?
I know hearsay can undo a kingdom.
I never cursed your tower guards
& I dare translate their foofaraw.
I double swear on the good book
though I could be our Shagspere
or William Kempe paying his tab
with a proud penny & a plug nickel.
Your Highness, only a horsewhip
could heal my unnatural tongue,
that is, if you consent to be the first
flogged up & down the castle steps.
After the guillotine & a coronation,
you would think a king too weak

to properly father a son & heir,
in the unholy days of the masque.
My queen, today, my lovely queen
singing wildly behind an iron door,
her head ready for your oak block,
holds now her lame bird in a box
of twigs, a toy against eternity.

THE RAVEN MASTER

Their feathers glisten wet light
in gauzy dark, their language
older than millet, gruel, ash pit,
& curses. Poe had to leave my tongue
before I became the keeper
of good omens. They go on talking
among themselves, but if I say
a few holy tropes of *Beowulf*
they listen, as if understanding
each ragged dactyl, even when
I speak in Grendel's voice.
They look at me & hop closer,
their eyes dark & true, shiny
as onyx. They laugh if I laugh.
Do they know my words
blessed warships afloat
& christened a stout prince?
Here, below the tower clock
across from the rookery
I offer them what I eat.

But the bloody damn lot
refuse my sunflower seeds
& tidbits from the royal table.
They only praise a hunk of raw meat
on a pointed sappy green stick.

THE KING'S SALT

The miners dressed in monkish garb
    led horses deep into briny catacombs
hewn by ancient rain. The horses crunched
    green apples while paced through a maze
of looped ropes, & the huge wooden pulleys
    & winches began to groan, moving blocks
& barrels of salt. The men were handpicked
    by the king, & the dark horses soon forgot
the pastures, walking circles, never to know
    the horizon again, wet grass under hooves.
If a miner died at home in bed beside his wife
    could another hand holding an apple or two
draw the horse into the rote, winding circle,
    obedient & unthinking? The penitents
held long poles with flame to burn off methane
    in the ceiling, the others pushed daylong
squat carts called the Hungarian dog.
    Faces & shapes rose from the monolith.
Here's a gnome, the guardian of miners,
    & this St. Kinga's Chapel, chandeliers
hanging—carved from a threefold silence.
    Wooden gutters drained off centuries

before shadows of German warplanes
    floated on the lakes of brine, hidden
by imperial weather. Now one stands
    wondering if a king, for the hell of it,
touched royal crystals with his tongue
    down in the dank half-darkness,
or gazed within, to have seen firsthand
    the moment when one carefully places
a small lamp behind a bust of salt.

LEMONS

Three or four in a sailor's pocket
or even one hidden in the corner
of a duffel bag may be life or death
on the high seas, lost in trade winds
ripping sails to tatters, Neptune's
night & day beaten into splintered
wood festooned in hard winds.
Now, a whiny ghost ship rides
nothing but its own oblivion
ahead, the souring mush & salt fish
in the raw bellies of the seamen,
hardly a tallyho in their stormy heads—
a rupture & burning in the gut,
but two or three days is forever
here beneath a ransacked sky,
& one lemon is big as the sun
rising out of tropical waters.

TURNER'S GREAT

TUSSLE WITH WATER

As you can see, he first mastered light
& shadow, faces moving between grass
& stone, the beasts wading to the ark,
& then *The Decline of the Carthaginian
Empire*, before capturing volcanic reds,
but one day while walking in windy rain
on the Thames he felt he was descending
a hemp ladder into the galley of a ship,
down in the swollen belly of the beast
with a curse, hook, & a bailing bucket,
into whimper & howl, into piss & shit.
He saw winds hurl sail & mast pole
as the crewmen wrestled slaves dead
& half-dead into a darkened whirlpool.
There it was, groaning. Then the water
was stabbed & brushed till voluminous,
& the bloody sharks were on their way.
But you're right, yes, there's still light
crossing the divide, seething around
corners of the thick golden frame.

SPERM OIL

Housed in a boom of blubber
& bone, harpooned six times,
the giant grew into a dynamo
hitched to six taut rope-lines
skipping the boat across waves
toward the blurry lighthouse.

It bled out a long silence
but men in oilskins labored
with hydraulics of light
on water, walked its flank,
& tore it down to a storeroom
of Nantucket scrimshaw.

Ballast stone or sledge?
They bashed in the skull
& lowered down the boy
to haul up buckets of oil
for candles that burned
a slow, clean, white glow.

At ten, he was almost a man
whose feet sank into the waxy
muck of ambergris. His sweat
dripped into a long hour.
Big as a barrel, the head
echoed a temple nave.

NOCTURNAL HOUSES

The animals seem to be gazing at a man's sky-blue trousers,
or they're looking at the fake stars bleeding through the floating
    mesh,
or they're distracted by the sheer smallness of a voice in a polka-
    dot dress,
or they're hypnotized by their own blood-polished paws, teeth, &
    snouts,
or they know when the hunter's great-grandson has entered their
    weather,
smiling, & they're intimidated by the Looney Tunes in his noble
    head.

*

See behind & ahead at the same time
& enter the tomb as the chosen one
with his trowel & bucket of wet mortar.
The venerated has been wrapped in gauze
dipped & dried in everlasting fluids,
surrounded by his earthly treasures.
Here comes the final light of tallow

& sacred incense, & then the ravenous,
all-knowing eyes of the cats circle
the squared dimension of the gateway
as he wedges in the last three stones
to seal out the longing of the world.

AUGURY AT SUNSET

The albino family on the other side
of the bean field—one son black
as his father, two daughters & another
son pale as their mother—all six
clustered around an upturned cable-stool
in the backyard beneath a chinaberry.

In that four-room brick-sided house,
what did it mean to close one's eyes
& see country laughter a half mile,
how it rises up & shimmies the air
till a cicada answers a goatsucker
from a muddy patch of cattails?

Maybe they talked old remedies
as African as their faces, saying,
If you wish a cure try a handful
of gum moss, a thimble of aniseed,
a handful of corn shucks, & steep
in a quart of rainwater. Drink at sunrise.

Back then thrashers wounded maypop.
The hounds barked. A crow on a fencepost
told us how to keep a cat at home
by feeding her sugar at seven o'clock
before rubbing grease on her paws
& bending her face to kiss a mirror.

Their affection was true as molasses,
the aroma of collards, green tomatoes,
chicken, cornbread, & peach ice cream
at twilight. Their shadows rose to walk
through pine woods, & I heard them
singing names of the restless dead.

SKULKING ACROSS SNOW

The shadow knows. Okay. But what is this, the traveler's tail curled like a question mark, a tribe on her back? Snow falls among the headstones. The fat flakes curtain three worlds. In Southern folklore, they exhume the old world before skulking out to a new frontier of city lights. They live by playing dead. Bounty of lunacy. Bounty of what it seems. No, I'm not talking about lines stolen into a rock 'n' roll song. No, arch sentimentalist, I'm not speaking of moonlight or a girl of wanderlust in a desert. But that's not a bad guess. I'm lost in your obscure imagination. Speaking of the dead, you know, Yeats also knew a little something about the occult. Sleepwalking is another story. Yes, the blank space says, Wake up, knucklehead, & listen to this: You might be getting onto something here. If I had different skin, would you read me differently, would you see something in the snow that isn't in the snow, something approaching genius? Would you press your nude body against the pages & try reading something into the life of the speaker? Would you nibble at the edges of my nightmares, & wake with the taste of death in your mouth, or would you open your eyes, lost in a field of hyacinth? Well, on a night like this, snow has fallen into my dreams. Lithium or horse could be a clue, but not necessarily so. Or, think of the two men aiming their dueling pistols—the years of silence between them—Alexander Pushkin falling into the January whiteness of history.

SPRUNG RHYTHM

OF A LANDSCAPE

Charles, I'm also a magpie collecting every scrap
of song, color, & prophecy beside the river
in the lonesome valley, along the Trail of Tears,
switchbacks, demarcation lines, & railroad tracks,
over a ridge called the Devil's Backbone,
winding through the double-green of Appalachia
down to shady dominion & Indian summer.
I don't remember how many times,
caught between one divine spirit & the next
detour, I wanted to fly home the old way,
around contours of doubt, tailspins
I'd learned to gauge so well, voices
ahead, before, not yet born, & beyond,
doubling back to the scent of magnolia.
Whatever it was in the apparitional light
held us to the road. But your early sky
was different from mine, as I drifted up
from bottomland, snagged by grab-vines
& bullfrog lingo in a bluesy grotto. One way
or another, a rise & fall is a rise & fall, a way in
& a way out, till we're grass danced-down.
I, too, know my Hopkins (Lightnin' & Gerard Manley),

gigging to this after-hours when all our little civil wars
unheal in the body. I shake my head till snake eyes fall
on the ground, as history climbs into the singing skull
to ride shotgun. Our days shaped by unseen movement
in the landscape, cold-cocked by brightness coming
over a hill, wild & steady as a palomino runagate
spooked by something in the trees unsaid.
The redbud followed us into starless cities
& shook us out like dusty rags in a dizzy breeze.
But we're lucky we haven't been shaken down
to seed-corn in a ragged sack, looped & cinched tight,
lumps of dirt hidden in our coat pockets.
Charles, we came as folk songs,
blues, country & western, to bebop & rock 'n' roll,
our shadows hanging out bandaged-up & drawn
on a wall easing into night melody of "Po' Lazarus"
at the top & the bottom of day. Each step taken,
each phrase, every snapped string, fallen arch,
& kiss on a forgotten street in Verona or Paris
transported us back—back to hidden paths,
abandoned eaves, & haylofts where a half century
of starlings roosted, back to when we were lost
in our dream-headed, separate eternities,
searching till all the pieces fit together,
till my sky is no bluer than your sky.

ROCK ME, MERCY

The river stones are listening
because we have something to say.
The trees lean closer today.
The singing in the electrical woods
has gone dumb. It looks like rain
because it is too warm to snow.
Guardian angels, wherever you're hiding,
we know you can't be everywhere at once.
Have you corralled all the pretty wild
horses? The memory of ants asleep
in daylilies, roses, holly, & larkspur.
The magpies gaze at us, still
waiting. River stones are listening.
But all we can say now is,
Mercy, please, rock me.

ISLANDS

An island is one great eye
    gazing out, a beckoning lighthouse,
searchlight, a wishbone compass,
    or counterweight to the stars.
When it comes to outlook & point
    of view, a figure stands on a rocky ledge
peering out toward an archipelago
    of glass on the mainland, a seagull's
wings touching the tip of a high wave,
    out to where the brain may stumble.

But when a mind climbs down
    from its lone craggy lookout
we know it is truly a stubborn thing,
    & has to leaf through pages of dust
& light, through pre-memory & folklore,
    remembering fires roared down there
till they pushed up through the seafloor
    & plumes of ash covered the dead
shaken awake worlds away, & silence
    filled up with centuries of waiting.

Sea urchin, turtle, & crab
    came with earthly knowhow,
& one bird arrived with a sprig in its beak,
    before everything clouded with cries,
a millennium of small deaths now topsoil
    & seasons of blossoms in a single seed.
Light edged along salt-crusted stones,
    across a cataract of blue water,
& lost sailors' parrots spoke of sirens,
    the last words of men buried at sea.

Someone could stand here
    contemplating the future, leafing
through torn pages of St. Augustine
    or the prophecies by fishermen,
translating spore & folly down to taproot.
    The dreamy-eyed boy still in the man,
the girl in the woman, a sunny forecast
    behind today, but tomorrow's beyond
words. To behold a body of water
    is to know pig iron & mother wit.

Whoever this figure is,
    he will soon return to dancing
    through the aroma of dagger's log,

ginger lily, & bougainvillea,
between chants & strings struck
    till gourds rally the healing air,
& the church-steeple birds
    fly sweet darkness home.
Whoever this friend or lover is,
    he intones redemptive harmonies.

To lie down in remembrance
    is to know each of us is a prodigal
son or daughter, looking out beyond land
    & sky, the chemical & metaphysical
beyond falling & turning waterwheels
    in the colossal brain of damnable gods,
a Eureka held up to the sun's blinding eye,
    born to gaze into fire. After conquering
frontiers, the mind comes back to rest,
    stretching out over the white sand.

LATITUDES

If I am not Ulysses, I am
his dear, ruthless half brother.
Strap me to the mast
so I may endure night sirens
singing my birth when water
broke into a thousand blossoms
in a landlocked town of the South,
before my name was heard
in the womb-shaped world
of deep sonorous waters.
Storms ran my ship to the brink,
& I wasn't myself in a kingdom
of unnamed animals & totem trees,
but never wished to unsay my vows.
From the salt-crusted timbers
I could only raise a battering ram
or cross, where I learned God
is rhythm & spores. If I am
Ulysses, made of his words
& deeds, I swam with sea cows
& mermaids in a lost season,
ate oysters & poison berries

to approach the idea of death
tangled in the lifeline's slack
on that rolling barrel of a ship,
then come home to more than just
the smell of apples, the heavy oars
creaking the same music as our bed.

RUM, SODOMY, & THE LASH

With the same gall as when he brought
a case of Douro wine & a copper bathtub
to the edge of battle, Churchill mocked
the Royal Navy, which stood a fortnight
caught in the sway of buckets,
as if they hadn't fought for their lives.
Men gazed at a fugitive horizon
with hands slanted over eyes,
pulled by distant ports of call
till drunken laughter covered
the dreadnought's oily deck.
Who knows what wild tempest
a few erotic drawings on silk
could conjure for men at sea.
With the thunderous waves
rousing memories in the brig,
sailors did not speak of thirst
or bread after teaching a parrot
to mourn loneliness in falsetto
along the coastline of Gallipoli.

THE RELIC

In Saint Helena darkness falls into a window.
Napoleon tells the doctor to cut out his heart
& send it to the empress, Marie-Louise,

but not one word is said about his penis.
Had an auctioneer or bibliophile known
the weight or the true cost of infamy?

After his body was shipped home for burial
in a great hall of clocks & candelabra
few could reign over imperial silence.

One was Vignali, paid in silver forks, knives,
& 100,000 francs to curate the funeral,
whose manservant, Ali, confessed the deed.

Now, we ask time to show us the keepsake,
to let us see the proof in blue morocco
& velvet locked in a glass case.

I wonder if the urologist in Englewood,
New Jersey, wrapped it in raw silk
& placed the talisman under his bed.

Or if it became a study for a master of clones
rehearsing doxology & transubstantiation,
not even a murmur covered by swanskin.

It's a hint of the imagination awakened,
a shoelace, a dried-up fig or seahorse
awaiting the gallop of soundless waves.

IL DUCE'S VILLA

Mussolini took his mistresses
there, where everything's built
to outlast a plunder of secret clocks,
& now newlyweds rent his bed for luck.

But one would think this ritual
sours the sweetest love apples
as rosewater turns to vinegar
& all doubt is left black & blue.

I can still see those Africans
selling knock-off sunglasses
& watches for upright middlemen
hidden in the everyday light.

In a square people throw rocks
at two ghosts hanging upside down.
Fano is now a half hour away,
& the engineer grips his brake.

Every tree here is a magician.
There's a country in the young
women & men at tall windows
set in stone, but maybe their bodies

try too hard to answer D'Annunzio's
lore of dead shepherds. As the train
speeds into a tyranny of frescoes
breathless coloration & depth

take hold, the blanched villa
in my head. Newlyweds tangled
in linen slow as a dream of egrets
clouding Ethiopia's brown Coptic hills.

ET TU, BRUTUS?

They left the Second City
after years of stand-up & improv,
& came here to search faces
in crowds, on boulevards
& subways, & audition
for roles at a level of slow
pain that pulled them apart,
though they both perfected
Jerry & Peter before learning
betrayal doesn't always taste
like metal. Walking the same
street, one went to Red Hook
to live in a fifth-floor walk-up
where he burned sandalwood,
& the other to a girlfriend
he met on the set of a soap
living across from Central Park.
They would see each other
at galleries in SoHo & Chelsea,
& joke about days of free wine
& bread, or meet in a lobby
or the toilet at the Public,

reading the faintest graffiti
over the urinal, & one wanted
to point out to the other how
it was usually the businessman
in a suit or Judas in a top hat
who didn't wash his hands.
They were in *King of Thieves*
on HBO, but one fell in love
with Jack Daniel's & the other
began working comedy clubs,
& seldom spoke of life & death
floating between them. One
afternoon in mid-September
they sat across from each other
in Washington Square Park
as strangers strolled & a quartet
played "My Favorite Things,"
& one said to himself, No,
that can't be him, because
he's two years older than me,
& the second said to his mutt,
I knew the day would come
when one of us sees the other
dead on a foreign street.

THE GOLD PISTOL

There's always someone who loves gold
bullion, boudoirs, & bathtubs, always
some dictator hiding in a concrete culvert
crying, Please don't shoot, a high priest
who mastered false acts & blazonry,
the drinking of a potion after bathing
in slow oils of regret, talismans, & amulets
honed to several lifetimes of their own,
the looting of safes & inlaid boxes of jewels,
moonlight on brimstone, fires eating sky,
& this is why my heart almost breaks
when a man dances with Gaddafi's pistol
raised over his head, knowing the sun
runs to whatever shines, & as the young
grows old, there's always a raven
laughing on an iron gatepost.

FACES AT THE WINDOW

They must be having fun down there,
Sarah sucking on all three colors
of her lollipop & Bruno looping out
his spinning top. Their laughter
rises up to slowly torture me.
They must be having fun. Yes,
Mother, I'm practicing my scales.

With Bruno gone years in the war
& Sarah lost over in America,
I've counted the green leap years.
Now the concert hall is filling up,
awaiting the prodigy to play rain
on a zinc roof. I'm in the first row
before I step out into the evening.

Those fingers on the keys unknot
my stitches. I knew all the notes
before a sparrow was condemned
to sing in the eaves. I stand here
motionless, clearly nothing but
a silhouette gazing at a ball
bouncing on the sidewalk.

He must be having fun. My days
just a touch-up of muted hues
& forgotten cadenzas. Somebody
please remember me. Sarah,
wherever you are, I hope
you're having fun. Ha-ha
still runs past my window,

down the hill. The dead live
across the street, up & down
our block. Oh, well, yes,
the piano. That's my son,
Federico, named after a great
Spanish poet, playing the keys
low as wind through blood weed.

CAFÉ DU RAT MORT

Tonight I'm ensconced
in Second Empire décor,
& it's good I followed my mind.

The automaton in a glass dome
holds my undivided attention—
a monkey smoking a cigarette.

It's more than a sprung blade
in the little assassin's shiny dagger
for the emperor's bastard son.

Rimbaud says to Verlaine,
"Please hold out your hand—
I wish to show you my experiment."

I can't believe it, but here comes
Fleur de Pipe, talking to herself
about how the moon brought her to Balzac.

Those two from the Isle of Lesbos
kissing beneath the Japanese print
are in my next graphic novel.

But I can't draw you a Bugatti
unless Isadora's luminous scarf
floats behind her like a comet.

All we need is another tall decanter
of ice water & the green glow of absinthe
poured over a lump of sugar.

THE CIRCUS

A war's going on somewhere, but tonight
a forest glows beneath the big top,
calling for the sword swallower & contortionist,
the beautiful high-wire walker who almost dies
nightly, the fire eater, the lion tamer, the believer
of sage & sleeping salts who wears a money belt
against her Icelandic skin. A drunk wants to be healed
by contagious laughter or a shot through the heart
by an old lover who lives in King of Prussia.
Three months ago, before Caldonia's body
was found by the police in waist-high weeds,
birds sang here. Maybe her killer is now
throwing a baseball to knock a dummy
into the water barrel, or buying cotton candy
for his daughter, or circling a bull elephant.
Who can remember the woman, the sirens,
her mother fainting next to this beaten tree?
Nighthawks work a lit thread through the evening.
The calliope makes the air tinny.
The strongman presses six hundred pounds,
his muscles flexed for the woman
whose T-shirt says THESE GUNS ARE LOADED.

But one minute later he's on the ground,
a petite bystander giving him mouth-
to-mouth. A cop blows his shiny whistle,
trying to clear a path for the paramedics.
Teenagers slurp root beer floats
& munch corn dogs, after they've leaned
into each other's arms in the flipped-over,
high-spinning rides, & have fallen in love
for the second time in three weeks.

MINOTAUR

He circled the roundabout
of bullheaded desires, lost in the maze
among broken icons, traces of blood
& sunflower seed left on numbered stones.

He was taller than a man,
tall as a honey locust at the end of an alley.
He slipped a knot, a sword at the equinox,
& entered the village plaza, hooking the air
& wheeling in circles.

The night dropped her cape,
& then artisans were ordered
to strike the figure onto a coat of arms
& gold coins. His cock & nose ring.
The triple-six tattooed on his rump.
Roses etched their scent on the night.

DEAR PANDORA

In your litany of glass boxes
within boxes, I can't believe
the alleys & cul-de-sacs,
how easily I get turned around
in my head. Yes, I'm no Solomon
hidden under a low glass bridge
built to reveal beauty's goatness
beneath garments of gold lamé
& silk breathing light. Foolkiller
that I am, I still have no doubt
you're God-sent. City of mood
swings & paradoxes, I've fallen
for a breezy nonchalance, your way
with words, basement jazz clubs
echoing voices of Trane & Elvin,
& those clusters of fat grapes
sighing in crystal wineglasses
at the Blue Hour. Honey,
you know, to tell you the truth,
I think I love your labyrinth.

TRANSFERENCE & BLING

Snow flares the gray morning at the bus stop.
It's damn cold, but the man's gold teeth
flash at the woman who stares down the boulevard,
plugged into her metallic-blue earphones,
painful hooped earrings stealing her glow.
A plated image from the "3rd hour"
dangles on a chain around his neck,
& the gilded weather in Tut's tomb
opens behind my eyelids. A door ajar.
A stone removed. A room light wounds.
The boy emperor & his treasures undisturbed.
The gold coffin inside a wooden coffin.
Dismantled chariots await charioteers, & centuries
reverse. "Where's our ride, bitch?" Is he talking to me,
the woman, or himself? The cold works on him,
icy knives whittling down the man his mama wanted.

SCRIMMAGE

Trees stand ready for snow & ice
slanting over far hills. An eagle coin
flipped at the blue hour spins double-
headed. Fall's imperial purples bloody
the rival battle gear for the pigskin.
After big steaks & imaginary girlfriends,
proxy platoons hunker under helmets
like loggerheads in wishbone & pistol
formations, ready for lightning to strike
or randy billy goats to butt heads. Honor
& dishonor touch lightly as the fans cheer.
The return of every nagging in the head
sits at the base of the spine wound tight
as a mainspring of bone & gut, the hum
of silent centuries till the ball is snapped.
The peacocks spread their tail feathers
on the sidelines of the sweaty gridiron,
hurrahing each touchdown & field goal
in the percussive air, running in place
every second left on a brutal clock.

IRONWORK

Strip the beached leviathan to ropy
muscle, bone, & ribbed heft,
unlatching everything that holds
the whole floating machine
struck dead by hunger at the shoreline.

Measure the bodacious shape
down to its last cubic foot
of oily silence, how its curved ribs
could hold three or four big men
if the dream of space is true.

Raise something new in the name
of this being showing us how
to tool a ship or submarine,
the blown song of wet stardust
pluming out of a blowhole.

From timbers curving into a boat
to raised arches of a cathedral,
& then to the steel cross-work
up there where it must tremble
to hold itself together down here.

One big embrace peaks & stops
in midair. Small things fit together
when a man loves his hands so much
we have to talk him down rung by rung
till his steel-toed boots touch the ground.

COMMON WEALTH

After trench warfare rolled
over Europe the scent of nitrate
& mustard gas hung in valleys
& avarice drifted into dance halls.

Treaties were signed & embossed
around rectangular inlaid tables,
new maps & demarcation lines
drawn on the reddish horizon.

Some estates, manor houses,
& castles were gutted, blown up
& carted off & dynamite
cast a gray skein over rivers.

For a while, they only knighted
robber barons with regal noses
& an inexhaustible love
for Henry James & Hollywood.

Some fun-loving guys & gals
jitterbugged in the Jazz Age
sold for sips of champagne
kisses in the Kit Kat Club.

Some of the bovine newcomers
were gifted in weekend soirees
& dinner parties. Fat scenarios
on temptation arrived in boxes.

Ah, she's in his world above hers,
his thick hands at the base
of her spine, true & strong
as a man beneath her class.

Fred Astaire foxtrots a fortnight,
& in a grand house of stone & gilt
someone may whisper a request
for a room across from another

someone whose father shot grouse
shooed from thickets of sage,
& who amassed his fortune
in bootlaces, war rations, & twine.

TORSION

He was in waist-high grass. An echo of a voice
    searched for him as he crawled along a ditch,
the greenhorn's blood reddening the mud, & the scent
    of burnt Cosmoline. *What's the spirit of the bayonet,*
soldier? His mind the mouth of a cave, the horizon
    was nitrate as he walked on his hands,
a howl in the crosshairs, rain tapping his helmet.
    He had been tapered, honed, & polished in AIT,
& then pointed toward grid coordinates on a ragged map,
    his feelings cauterized, & now a glint of wet light
touches the sniper's rifle in a grove of jackfruit.
    Silence, a stone in his belly, an anvil on his head.
What's the spirit of the bayonet, soldier? He dove on the pig
    & his body became part of the metal, tracer rounds
scorched the living air, the dirt & sky, & the edges of night
    approached. Only his fingers would recall threading
another belt of ammo. He didn't wish to know how many
    shadows hugged the ground. No, he couldn't stop
firing as he rode the M60 machine gun to a primal grunt
    before he buckled & spewed vomit over the barrel,
the torsion a whiplash of hues. *What's the spirit*
    of the bayonet, soldier? After medevac choppers

flew out the badly wounded & the body bags,
       three men in his squad became two tigers at sunset
& walked through the village. They kicked a pagoda
       till it turned into the crumbly dust of cinnabar,
& then torched thatched roofs. The captain's citation
       never said how fear tussled him in the paddy ditch,
& the star in its velvet-lined box was a scarab
       in a pharaoh's brain. The dead visited nightly.
The company chaplain blessed him, but he'd sit hours
       gazing out at the sea & could never bless himself.
The battalion saluted but he wished to forget his hands,
       & the thought of metal made him stand up straight.
He shipped back to the world only to remember blood
       on the grass, men dancing on a lit string of bullets,
women & children wailing among the flame trees,
       & he wished he hadn't been trained so damn well.
What's the spirit of the bayonet, soldier? He was back
       now, back to where he brandished fronds as swords
to guard their tree house, his mama at church
       singing hallelujah, his daddy in Lucky's
swigging Falstaff. He kept thinking of his cousin Eddie
       who drove his girl to Galveston in a Chevy pickup,
"California Dreamin'" looping through the cab.
       He could still see round fishing boats on the edge
of the South China Sea, a woman's long black hair
       falling in a rising wave, moonlight on the skin

of sappers, their bodies wound in concertina.
    He switches off his blue transistor radio
& walks straight into pines along the Black Warrior,
        searching for arrowheads, bagging rabbit & quail.
He's back to the Friday his draft card came, when he first
        mastered a willful blindness, back to outsmarting prey,
& he duckwalks across the clearing under power lines.
    Now ashamed of something naked as a good question
redbirds flash in a counter ambush. *Thou shalt not kill*
        echoes across clay hills miles from his loved ones,
& he slouches deeper into the Choctaw's old growth,
        through a hoop of light, away from a face stealing
his brother's, so deep he can hardly hear himself plead
        to shiny crows in a weeping willow.

ALWAYS A WAY

There's an echo of Chuck Berry's guitar
saying, "As I was motivatin' over the hill
I saw Maybelline in a Coupe de Ville . . ."
Wildflowers have sprung up along
the roadside bearing the agony
of being alive on a day bright as this.
Every good thing we dared in winter
arrives by springtime: a whippoorwill
among the pines, a colony of memories
like muscadine on a vine double thick
as a boy's arm, redemption reaching
into its roots before an afterthought
steals back the sweetness. Something
lost in the rearview mirror shifts,
& here we are again on the dance floor
at the Silver Shadow, the boys & girls
reeling out to the edge of fingertips.

A new feeling runs its live wire
through the air a few months before
James Dean fails to straighten out
a curve somewhere in California.

"Maybelline, why can't you be true?"
The flowers always find a way
into alleys & gullies, up to the shaded
woods where darkness plays God,
into the ordinary lives of women
& men, till *The Potato Eaters*
doesn't remind them of family
anymore. Something's about
to happen in blue, a stolen note
on the cusp, or chords struck
across the abyss. No, don't worry,
the sun always finds some way
to herd aster up into the rocks.

FORTRESS

Now I begin with these two hands
held before me as blessing & weapon,

blackbirds in fierce flight & instruments
of touch & consolation. This sign means

stop, & this one of course means come forth,
friend. I draw a circle in the red iron clay

around my feet, where no evil spirit dares
to find me. One's hands held at this angle

over a boy's head are a roof over a sanctuary.
I am a greenhorn in my fortress in the woods

with my right eye pressed to a knothole.
I can see a buzz in the persimmon tree,

its ripe letting go—a tiny white cross
in each seed. The girl's fiery jump rope

strikes the ground. I see the back door
of that house close to the slow creek

where a drunken, angry man stumbles
across the threshold every Friday.

I see forgiveness, unbearable twilight,
& these two big hands know too much

about nail & hammer, plank & uneasy sky.
Hewn stone & mortar is another world,

& sometimes a tall gate comes first.
Then huge wooden barrels of grain,

flour, salted meat, & quicklime before
twenty-eight crossbows in four towers.

LONGITUDES

Before zero meridian at Greenwich
Galileo dreamt Dante on a ship
& his beloved Beatrice onshore,
both holding clocks, drifting apart.

His theory was right even if
he couldn't steady the ship
on rough seas beyond star charts
& otherworldly ports of call.

"But the damn blessed boat
rocked, tossing sailors to & fro
like a chorus of sea hags
in throes of ecstasy."

My whole world unmoors
& slips into a tug of high tide.
A timepiece faces the harbor—
a fixed point in a glass box.

You're standing on the dock.
My dreams of you are oceanic,
& the Door of No Return
opens a galactic eye.

If a siren stations herself
between us, all the clocks
on her side, we'll find each other
sighing our night song in the fog.

DAYTIME BEGINS WITH A LINE BY ANNA AKHMATOVA

The round, hanging lanterns,
lit faces in a window of the Marble Palace
Catherine the Great built for a lover,
with the Field of Mars below,
snow falling inside two minds.
One translated Babylonian folktales
so the other could stand in line early morning
for bread at the House of Scholars.
A touch of dawn was again nightfall,
their room furnished with scattered papers,
rare books, a couch with springs poking out,
a bookcase, a floral pitcher, a china cabinet,
a naked lightbulb dangling over a table.
Did the two poets learn it took more
to sing & reflect the burning icy stars
of poetry where privilege & squalor
lived beneath the same ornate ceiling?
Did they tiptoe from the wintery dusk
of the servants' wing, follow the pseudo-
Gothic stairs up to the forbidden aromas

of Turkish tobacco, sugar, & exotic teas?
Sometimes, they kept themselves warm
with talk of the empress's love of horses
as they galloped another century. Then,
sketches of their time at the Stray Dog
lit the air around those neoclassic nights,
& maybe they also spoke about "Venice
rotting with gold" near the Arctic Circle,
& anger almost kept them warm on days
they bent over pages of snow blindness
where tears brought them to laughter.

MICHIO ITO'S FOX & HAWK

Ito ran to a window. He danced.
He howled. He cursed the moon,
interned in a camp before he was
carted on a ship back to Tokyo.
Hadn't he almost died for art
the evenings he ate bread soup?
If he wished to forget those days
& nights dancing in drawing rooms
in London, or translating Fenollosa's
notes on Noh, he'd have to unbraid
himself from *At the Hawk's Well*,
& then let go of the Egyptian
mask Dulac painted him into—
claws, beak, feathers, & legend.
Why did that silly boy tell a story
about his grandmother weeping
when she first saw him dressed
in his grandfather's samurai armor
to hold the gaze of Lady Cunard?
He was again studying the fox
holding a biscuit in his hand,
saying, "I went to a great hill

in Hampstead & I made my soul
into the soul of the fox." Finally,
he would let go of his Europe,
& not think of those he loved
& taught, Isadora lost. Now,
powerless & alone, he dances
his ten steps again & again,
wanting to know if a hawk
could peck the eyes out of a fox.

CAFFE REGGIO

They clink glasses of Merlot & joke
in a meta-language among friends
about early autumn in a gulag
of lonely washes. Then one says,
Ivan the Terrible was a teenage vampire
who fell in love with art & soothsayers,
& another says, If he had only ridden
a gondola through the canals of Venice
once or twice, they could have civilized
the madman dreaming of the Baltics.
Then, one of them says something
about sentimentality being the death
of imagination, metaphor, & foreplay.
They are one small republic of ideas,
three good friends, & almost one mind
when they lift their eyes to greet
a woman walking in from the day's
blinding array of disorder & chance.
She finds a table at the corner window,
orders a bowl of fruit & cappuccino,
opens a copy of *Watermark*, presses

down the pages, breaking the spine.
The three sit, smiling at each other,
& Derek says, I wonder if she knows
Joseph still picks up his mail here.

PRAISE BE

When the trees were guilty, hugged up
to history & locked in a cross-brace
with Whitman's Louisiana live oak,
you went into that mossy weather.

Did you witness the shotguns at Angola
riding on horseback through the tall sway
of sugarcane, the glint of blue steel
in the bloodred strawberry fields?

Silence was backed up in the cypress,
but you could hear the birds of woe
singing praise where the almost broken-
through sorrow rose from the deep woods

& walked out into moonshine as the brave
ones. You went among those who had half
a voice, whose ancestors mastered quicksand
by disappearing. Maybe our paths crossed

ghosts hogtied in the wounded night,
but it is only now I say this: Galway,
thanks for going down into our fierce hush
at the crossroads to look fear in the eye.

KRAR

We have this to call to the dead
among the living, this wooden triangle,
its belly a gourd-resonator
the size of a man's cupped hands
inverted, in prayer & war.
It throws sorrow & laughter
against the eardrum
till the silent motion of the hills
finds us in the city.
Water trembles at the taproot
when strings are struck,
reaching down through muscle memory
to a shelter of mud bricks baked under
three thousand years of sunlight,
from the goatherd to the King
of Kings, to Bob Marley. If Ethiopia
opens in the long Egyptian trumpets
or natural blues of the saxophone,
there's little pomp & circumstance
in this earthy instrument
raised between violin & crossbow,

to dance with, or embrace.
When it speaks, especially
to the drum, this sounding-loom
is the voice of a nation
bargaining with the gods.

DEAD RECKONING II

In a half-broken room of the hospice
the bent figure on a bed is far from Osibisa
or his twenty-four-hour rock 'n' roll gig
in England. Now, fame is a tale mermaids
tell fishermen, but all I want to know is
where are Kiki Djan's friends & lovers,
his millions? His eyes stop us at the foot
of the bed. Outside, migratory birds
fly in the shape of a falling garment.
He hugs a tape recorder, head swaying
to an unreleased recording cut overseas.
The hum of an insect can hold his gaze
for hours, the ancestors at a side door.
The song is his only possession, fingers
on the keyboard only a little howl lost
in a trade wind nudging a pirate ship.
His eyes tell us all the tangled paths
taken, & now he must be a Lindbergh
who crossed the sleepless Atlantic.
To fully master out-of-body travel
by dead reckoning, one has to know

all the overtime shadows of obeah
working around the clock in Accra.
He stares at the buzz of a bluebottle
throbbing against the windowpane.

A NIGHT IN TUNISIA

How long have I listened
to this blues & how long
has Dizzy Gillespie been dead?
I remember an old longing,
a young man reaching
for luck, a finger poised
between pages of Baldwin's
Notes of a Native Son, a clock
stopped for a hard, crystal-
clear moment. This was
a lifetime before the night
streets of Tunisia burned
on cell phones in the clouds,
tear gas & machine-gun fire
& my head in my hands
an hour. I traveled there
many times, humble
side streets & sweetness
of figs, hot seasons of meat
on the bone, naked feeling,
& Dizzy's horn still ablaze,
a bleat of big fat notes

in the dark. Even if I'd never
stepped above simple laws,
my youth had betrayed me
with years still to come
& jasmine in bloom.

THE KING

He rolls in the grass to disguise
his scent, & drags himself to the edge
to wait out another night, an ox-pecker
on his back. Three shadows shift,
& shift again in the jacaranda.

They always know when he's near
his gully, his proud, unruly head
raised toward the sun cornered
in a blue wash of muted splendor
broken open by a flash of hooves.

The one on the right, the left,
the half-broken one in the middle,
which one, huh? If only his mane
could still cast fear over the valley,
if strength came back to his legs.

He could still see the lioness
tugging the zebra up an incline
of wildflowers to her pride,
only a look & her calm alert
keep him back from the kill.

After eating grass for days,
he squints his one good eye
to rule dusk for an hour or two
but refuses to ride down a gazelle
bowed at the watering hole.

Black flies swarm as the sun
sinks deeper into the mud.
He knows birth & armature,
but now in this perfect glum
his mouth is a busted lamp.

THE DAY I SAW
BARACK OBAMA READING
DEREK WALCOTT'S
<u>COLLECTED POEMS</u>

Was he looking for St. Lucia's light
to touch his face those first days
in the official November snow & sleet
falling on the granite pose of Lincoln?

If he were searching for property lines
drawn in the blood, or for a hint
of resolve crisscrossing a border,
maybe he'd find clues in the taste of breadfruit.

I could see him stopped there squinting
in crooked light, the haze of Wall Street
touching clouds of double consciousness,
an eye etched into a sign borrowed from Egypt.

If he's looking for tips on basketball,
how to rise up & guard the hoop,
he may glean a few theories about war
but they aren't in *The Star-Apple Kingdom*.

If he wants to finally master himself,
searching for clues to govern seagulls
in salty air, he'll find henchmen busy with locks
& chains in a ghost schooner's nocturnal calm.

He's reading someone who won't speak
of milk & honey, but of looking ahead
beyond pillars of salt raised in a dream
where fat bulbs split open the earth.

The spine of the manifest was broken,
leaking deeds, songs, & testaments.
Justice stood in the shoes of mercy,
& doubt was bandaged up & put to bed.

Now, he looks as if he wants to eat words,
their sweet, intoxicating flavor. Banana leaf
& animal, being & nonbeing. In fact,
craving wisdom, he bites into memory.

The President of the United States of America
thumbs the pages slowly, moving from reverie
to reverie, learning why one envies the octopus
for its ink, how a man's skin becomes the final page.

THE GREEN HORSE

The kneeling figure is from Yama or Carthage,
& I ask, What was his worth in gold, in salt,
spices, statuary, or commemorated axioms?
L, if we weren't brave enough to believe
we could master time, we wouldn't have
locked hands with old gods smelted down
in shops where crosses were etched above doors,
pressed into the coinage of a new empire,
& palm readers flogged in the market.
But of course there sits Marcus Aurelius
with stoic meditations on a borrowed tongue,
gazing out at sublime poppies, an eternal
battlefield, his hand extended as a scepter
over the piazza where his bronze horse
cantered up onto Michelangelo's pedestal
carved from marble steps of the temple
of Castor & Pollux, & we wait for him
to outflank the epochs of wind & rain.
L, everything around here is an epitaph.
Even the light. This morning, squinting out
a window as rays play off a stone cistern,
I hear someone whisper, "Waste no time

arguing about what a good man should be,
the worms will give us their verdict
by nightfall." I don't know who said this,
but today, love, I'm brave enough to say,
Antiquity, here's my barbarian shadow
squatting under the horse's raised right hoof.

ODE TO THE OUD

Gourd-shaped muse swollen
with wind in the mulberry,
tell me everything you're made of,
little desert boat of Ra.
Oblong box of Bedouin doves
pecking pomegranate seeds out of the air,
you're the poet's persona, his double
in the high priest's third chamber,
each string a litany of stars over the Sahara.
Pear-shaped traveler, strong but so light,
is there a wishbone holding you together?
I wish I knew how to open you up
with an eagle's feather or a pick
whittled from buffalo horn,
singing alive the dust of Nubia.
Rosewood seasoned long ago,
I wish I could close your twelve mouths
with kisses. Tongues strung in a row,
I wish I could open every sound in you.
I envy one blessed to master himself
by rocking you in his lonely arms.

Little ship of sorrow, bend your voice
till the names of heroes & courtesans,
birds & animals, prayers & love songs,
swarm from your belly.

WITH MY FISH-SKIN DRUM

I shall sing the caravan home again,
bone & muscle holding me together,
earth & sky beneath my feet,

my fingers on the tabla, a red lotus
opening into the Great Rift Valley
till I am called to the reed boats.

I shall sing the whiskered tern's
lament I stole for occidental nights
as villagers walk toward big cities.

The caravan swallows the dust
of those before, woven into a dance
caught in a glow of night fires,

& I hold to my drum, waking voices
under the singing skin, the shish & tap
of fish skin on waters of a lost road.

ENVOY TO PALESTINE

I've come to this one grassy hill
in Ramallah, off Tokyo Street,
to place a few red anemones
& a sheaf of wheat on Darwish's grave.
A borrowed line transported me beneath
a Babylonian moon & I found myself
lucky to have the shadow of a coat
as warmth, listening to a poet's song
of Jerusalem, the hum of a red string
Caesar stole off Gilgamesh's lute.
I know a prison of sunlight on the skin.
The land I come from they also dreamt
before they arrived in towering ships
battered by the hard Atlantic winds.
Crows followed me from my home.
My coyote heart is an old runagate
redskin, a noble savage, still Lakota,
& I knew the bow before the arch.
I feel the wildflowers, all the grasses
& insects singing to me. My sacred dead
is the dust of restless plains I come from,
& I love when it gets into my eyes & mouth

telling me of the roads behind & ahead.
I go back to broken treaties & smallpox,
the irony of barbed wire. Your envoy
could be a reprobate whose inheritance
is no more than a swig of firewater.
The sun made a temple of the bones
of my tribe. I know a dried-up riverbed
& extinct animals live in your nightmares
sharp as shark teeth from my mountains
strung into this brave necklace around
my neck. I hear Chief Standing Bear
saying to Judge Dundy, "I am a man,"
& now I know why I'd rather die a poet
than a warrior, tattoo & tomahawk.

TIMBUKTU

I sing an elegy for the city of 333 saints,
for every crumbling mosque & minaret,
for the libraries standing for centuries
against dust storms, for the nomads
herding trees of life across the desert
along trails where camels hauled salt
to rafts woven on the River Niger
before the empire of Songhai fell.
The griots speak of an epic memory
of stardust in sand, but now mercenaries
kidnap, run drugs, & kill in bold daylight.
Blood money brought them into Libya,
& more blood money took them home
brandishing stolen guns & grenades.
When Lord Byron intones in *Don Juan*
"Where geography finds no one to oblige her"
I hear my name. But no one stands up
to prophecies the other side of limbo
against the modern as a metallic eye
drones overhead. Medieval clouds
may promise safe passage or escape
routes out of Mali, but the God-fearing
cannot remember the faces of death
after kicking in all the drums.

MONOLITH

The faces of Pussy Riot
move through the crowd
on a placard in Kiev, mist
of breath & weather rising,
& then tear gas & bullets.

A chorus of protesters fall
dead in snow, the woman
still holding to her sign.
Okay, friend, we can talk
about Victor Hugo,

how tomorrow hides inside
yesterday, how an emperor
marked his name on air
as half-dead soldiers hid
in the bellies of horses.

But let's come back to vigils
burned out & flowers heaped
around Independence Square,
to the after-sound of rock bands
in the night's cold epitaph.

GHAZAL, AFTER FERGUSON

Somebody go & ask Biggie to orate
what's going down in the streets.

No, an attitude is not a suicide note
written on walls around the streets.

Twitter stays lockstep in the frontal lobe
as we hope for a bypass beyond the streets,

but only each day bears witness
in the echo chamber of the streets.

Grandmaster Flash's thunderclap says
he's not the grand jury in the streets,

says he doesn't care if you're big or small
fear can kill a man on the streets.

Take back the night. Take killjoy's
cameras & microphones to the streets.

If you're holding the hand lightning strikes
juice will light you up miles from the streets

where an electric chair surge dims
all the county lights beyond the streets.

Who will go out there & speak laws
of motion & relativity in the streets?

Yusef, this morning proves a crow
the only truth serum in the street.

INTERROGATION

He picks till it grows
into a tiny butterfly,
a transfigured bee-
shaped wound,
& then into a secret icon
filled with belief,
bloody philosophy,
& a drop of stardust.

A moment of half-
dead radiance
pulses on his skin
till his mouth closes
on a phrase in Latin,
& he wonders if an oath
leaves a scar.

He can't hear
the nightlong voice
recant in the bell tower,
or the wasp's torn wings
lifting hints of light
in the spider's web.

When thought is
tissue, or a string
of dust that sings for rain,
unforgivable hours
divide into testimonies
delivered by the wind,
saying, Forget.

He tries not to pick
at the mute evidence
of the recent past,
letting pop songs
bleed over him
on the radio.

He lifts the scab
with a fingernail,
till the almost healed
opens its little doubtful
mouth of resignation,
till he can gaze down
into himself & see
where eternity begins.

PRECIOUS METALS

After the MRI & robot
made of precious metals,
some heretical go-between
shouted all the tautologies
& fruitless apologies to the planet.
I came to you, saying, Please
look into my eyes & tap a finger
against my heart to undo
every wrong I've ever done,
every infraction done to me
in the country of crabapple
& honeysuckle. I want to
toy with each blade of grass
& ripening plum, to suck the
last salutation from doubt,
& mount a dancer's platform.
I've outlived silent seasons
whipped bloody & ransomed.
But let us ride the big wheel
into dawn, a naked kiss.
I say, If you wish to trouble

my persona or need to break
my bones to show me mercy,
then get on with your work
& fix me the way a Delta blues
fixes a muddy river's night sky.

THE ENCHANTED DIVER

We backflip from the skiff,
& ease down, down as if falling
into another, or into a deep cloud
of bubbles & weather of the self
where nightmares go, till a flange
catches & holds, married
to King Neptune's daughter.

We drift among the unnamed
& invade a world of annelid,
serpents, & fauna walking
into a cave to a crystal obelisk
& toppled limestone pyramid
as if descending azure columns
on the shoulders of Poseidon.

We sink into each other's reflection
on walls of an underwater museum.
Ancient feeling, ritual, & certainties
are nearly erased from stone reliefs,
& I'm a few feet inside the temple
of Iris, & my fingers ache to touch
any golden thing of Cleopatra's.

I swim eye-level to a sphinx
in a grand square cocked slant
by the gravity of long waiting,
thankful you have anchored me
here, & I see broken mirrors
of the Alexandrian lighthouse
lit by a school of cuttlefish.

I raise my hands to the mask,
my mouth half open, trembling
in the rage of the earth centuries
before. What was God thinking?
Now, I remember, this is how
I first almost died, learning to work
the inglorious fins on my feet.

A PRAYER

Great Ooga-Booga, in your golden pavilion
beside the dung heap, please
don't let me die in a public place.
I still see the man on the café floor
at the airport beneath a canopy
of fluorescence, somewhere
in the Midwest or back East,
travelers walking around him
& texting on cell phones
while someone shocked him back,
fiddling with dials & buttons
on a miraculous instrument.
Was the memory of a dress in his head?

Great Ooga-Booga, forgive me
for wearing out my tongue before
I said your praises. No, I haven't
mastered the didgeridoo.
I don't have an epic as a bribe.
My words are simple. Please
don't let me die gazing up at a streetlight
or the Grand Central facades.

Let me go to my fishing hole
an hour before the sun sinks
into the deep woods, or swing
on the front porch, higher & higher
till I'm walking on the ceiling.

THE WORK OF ORPHEUS

He blows a ram's horn at the first gate of the third kingdom, & one would swear it sounds like questions in the air. He walks down a troubadour's path that comes to a halt as if his song has broken in half, standing on cobblestones that stop before tall waves below. Whatever was here is now gone, except for a percussive whisper of mail & swords. He knows the sea is a keeper of records. Gazing up at the sun, he shakes his head & walks toward a refugee camp with a sack of beans, bread, dried tomatoes, & fish, where he plays "Hallelujah" on a toy trumpet. He knows they hate a bugle blown at dawn, or the sound of taps. A sloping path toward the center of town leads him to a prison made of river stones & thatch. The faces behind bars wait for him. Does he dare to raise his reed flute to his lips this mute hour? The sun sinks like a clarion, an old war cry across windy grass or questions in the air. He goes to the rear door of the slaughterhouse & plays his Pan fife till the flies go, as the workers speak of days they drank rosewater. He heads down along the creek's muddy bank, finds a fallen tree, sits, & raises the clay flute to his lips. A magpie lands on a branch a foot away. He stops playing, whispers to his messenger, Okay, now go out there & tell them.

EMPYREAN ISLES

We have gone there, sitting here
while Herbie plays water on stone,
his piano among the misty trees.
Rainy light flows over hillocks
beside the sea, leaves, & high grass,
underneath nighttime till the Egg
glows. A place becomes the shape
of one's mind, & secretive animals
encounter us sleepwalkers. Dawn
flows over round wooden cisterns
atop buildings as East River fog
journeys along the streets & avenues.
All the seasons crowd here at once,
& each has several minds. The boy
never leaves the middle of my life.
The firebirds eat clouds of insects
as black keys counter white keys,
& I beg you to sing me an old song.
I weigh love of fruit in both hands.
We're two halves of a struck bell.
The boy's here, his big jolly balloon
tugging me now & then off-balance.

You wake me, laughing in your sleep.
The roots are knotted underneath us.
The boy smiles, & then dares me to kiss
my left elbow. You are a double mirror
guarding me from city lights & free will,
& I'm too scared to let go of your voice
in a subkingdom of mist on the stones.
Damned if we do. Damned if we don't.
The LP spins nightlong on repeat.
The boy has my long, girlish eyelashes.

SPRINGTIME IN ATLANTIS

It always edges out of the corners
of hidden things this time of year
as damp green returns to the hills
& valley, working around what snow
& ice pulled down to wintry loam.
Every wild thing here buds & leafs,
& then the house of earth colors
with blue doors & trim eases closer.
The grape arbor woven around
toppled stone heads & pale busts
seems to hold the place together.
Today, it all stands out against sky
& the slow movement of women
& men carried by chores & songs
at this commune they call Atlantis.
The retired artists who live here
among wind chimes & birdbaths
work the garden spring & summer,
& in fall they bag & freeze the bounty
of snow peas, corn, squash, rutabaga,
& turnips. A quarter-acre burial plot
slopes down between the bass pond

& the sour-apple trees. They come
& go, always ten to fourteen around
the wide oak table where they sip
homemade wine & break daily bread.
After dessert, & the dishes washed,
they dance in each other's arms,
whisper to the dead, tell secrets,
swear allegiances, & fall in love.
A ballerina pirouettes around a Hamlet
on his knees, reciting a soliloquy
to a skull reflected on a windowpane.
A watercolorist raises his hands
& turns into a Gypsy troubadour
with a loon's lament in his throat.
Nightly, an unmerciful harmony
shakes the house as the sculptor
hugs anything of wood. For years
this place has been a paradise,
& if a passing stranger should jeer
their lewdness or the evening hills
betrayed by the scent of a pigsty,
they only say their sows are raised
to nourish the soil, the peacocks
are here to drop lovely feathers,
& the two goats eat the brambles.
They say oaths have been sworn

at the table. A few tattoos speak
legends. They say they're lovers,
not fighters, though Robin Hood
& the evil sheriff of Nottingham
occupy a few minds. Animals
pass through a wet darkness
to speed up the night. Mornings
& afternoons are one big straw hat.
At this hour, they call & play catch
among the hellebore & lungwort,
& are lucky to have never stopped
leaving a skeleton key in the lock.

NOTES

"Islands" and "The Day I Saw Barack Obama Reading Derek
Walcott's *Collected Poems*" were written to celebrate
Derek Walcott's eighty-first birthday with friends in St. Lucia.

"Sprung Rhythm of a Landscape" is for Charles Wright.

"Rock Me, Mercy" is in memory of the victims at Newtown.

"Praise Be" is in memory of Galway Kinnell.

"Dead Reckoning II" is in memory of Kiki Djan.

ACKNOWLEDGMENTS

Grateful acknowledgment is made to the following print
and digital publications, where some of these poems originally
appeared: *The American Poetry Review*, *The Believer*, *Black
Renaissance / Renaissance Noire*, *The Boston Review*, *Consequence*,
Europe, *The Fiddlehead*, *Free Verse*, *The Kenyon Review*, *LUMINA*,
The Moth, *The New Yorker*, *The Newtowner*, *The Northwest
Review*, NPR, *Obsidian*, *The Paris American*, *phati'tude*,
Plume, *PN Review*, *Poem-a-Day*, *Poems for Mamilla* (ARCH
pamphlet), *Poetry*, *Savvy*, *Slate*, *Tin House*, and *The Wolf*.